A
LET'S-READ-AND-FIND-OUT SCIENCE BOOK

STRAIGHT HAIR, CURLY HAIR

BY AUGUSTA GOLDIN   Illustrated by Ed Emberley

Is your hair straight? Is your hair curly? This cheerful book explains why, in simple, scientifically accurate language.

Mrs. Goldin tells how hair grows, why dampness makes straight hair straighter and curly hair curlier, why the characteristics of hair cannot be changed. Two easy experiments show how strong hair is and how it stretches.

Ed Emberley's rollicking illustrations combine with the easy-to-read text to make an enticing book on a subject that is sure to interest every curious child.

STRAIGHT HAIR, CURLY HAIR

BY AUGUSTA GOLDIN   ILLUSTRATED BY ED EMBERLEY

THOMAS Y. CROWELL
COMPANY
NEW YORK

This Crowell Crocodile is one of the quality paperback editions
selected from Crowell's highly recommended:

LET'S-READ-AND-FIND-OUT SCIENCE BOOKS

Editors: Dr. Roma Gans, Professor Emeritus of Childhood Education, Teachers College, Columbia University. Dr. Franklyn M. Branley, Astronomer Emeritus and former Chairman of the American Museum—Hayden Planetarium.

STRAIGHT HAIR, CURLY HAIR

Look at yourself in a mirror.
The top of your head is covered with hair.
Is your hair straight? Is it wavy?
Is your hair tight and curly?
What color is it?

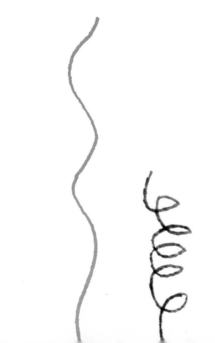

Straight, wavy, or curly, black or brown or red or blond, your hair keeps your head warm in winter. It protects your head from the sun in summer. It cushions your scalp against bumps and bruises, and it makes a frame for your face.

Right now there are about 100,000 hairs on your head.
Some hairs are growing.
Some hairs have finished growing and are ready to fall out.
When a hair falls out, a new one grows back in its place. You can't stop it from growing back.

Hair grows about half an inch a month, and it keeps growing until it reaches its natural length. This does not mean that your hair would naturally grow to the floor if you never cut it.

The natural length of your hair may be six inches, or ten inches, or more than fifteen inches.

This means your hair will only grow to its natural length. If the natural length of your hair is six inches, it will only grow to be six inches long.

If the natural length of your hair is ten or fifteen inches, your hair will only grow to be ten or fifteen inches long.

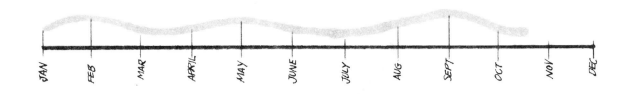

Some people have hair that grows so long, it reaches down to their knees.

Long or short, your 100,000 hairs grow out of 100,000 tiny holes in your scalp. These holes are called FOLLICLES.

A follicle may be round.
A follicle may be oval.
A follicle may be narrow like a little slot.

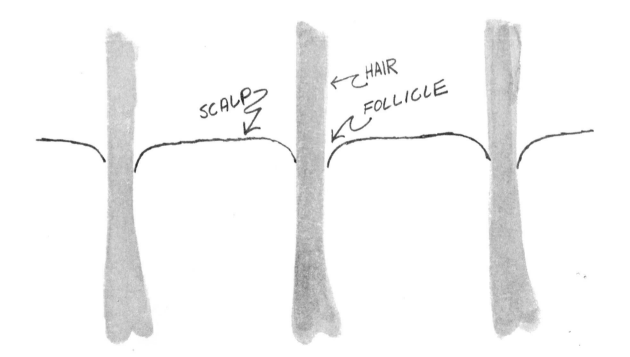

You can tell the shape of your follicles by looking at your hair.

If your hair is straight, your follicles are round.

If your hair is a little curly, you have oval follicles.

If your hair is very curly, you have follicles that are shaped like little slots.

14

If you looked at a slice of hair through a microscope, you would see that the shape of your hair matches the shape of your follicles. You would see that

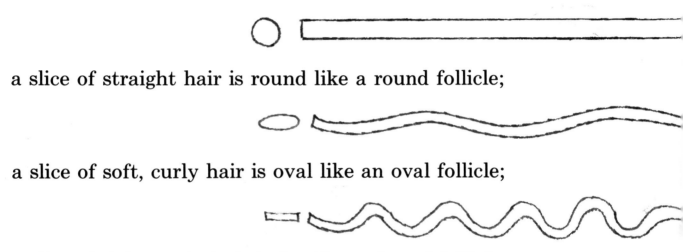

a slice of straight hair is round like a round follicle;

a slice of soft, curly hair is oval like an oval follicle;

a slice of tight, curly hair is flat like a slotted follicle.

You cannot change the shape of your hair because you cannot change the shape of your follicles. The kind of hair you have will always be the same.

Rub some hair gently between your fingers and listen.
You hear small, crackling sounds.

Even the smoothest hair makes these sounds. That's because every hair is covered with small, hard scales. You could see these scales with a microscope. You could see that they overlap like shingles on a roof. When you rub your hair, the scales catch onto each other. The small sounds you hear are the sounds of the scales grating together.

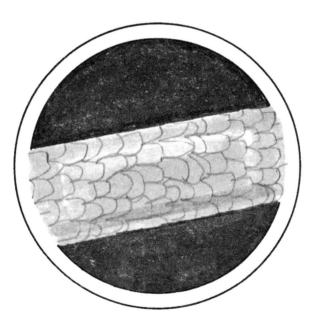

When the weather is cool and dry, the scales lie
 smooth on every hair.
When the weather is warm and damp, they rise up.
The moisture makes each hair swell and thicken.

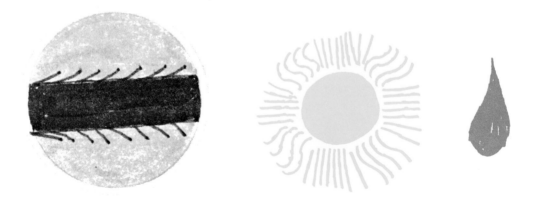

Straight hair swells and thickens and gets straighter.
Curly hair swells and thickens and gets curlier.
If you have naturally curly hair, your head may be
   covered with tight little ringlets on rainy days.

Straight or curly, black or brown, red or blond, your hair is very strong, and you can prove this.

Take a long hair, some Scotch tape, and a twelve-inch ruler. Tape one end of the hair to the ruler, and tape the other end to the rod in your clothes closet. Watch. The hair will not break. That ruler may swing there for a week, and if no one disturbs it, the hair will not break.

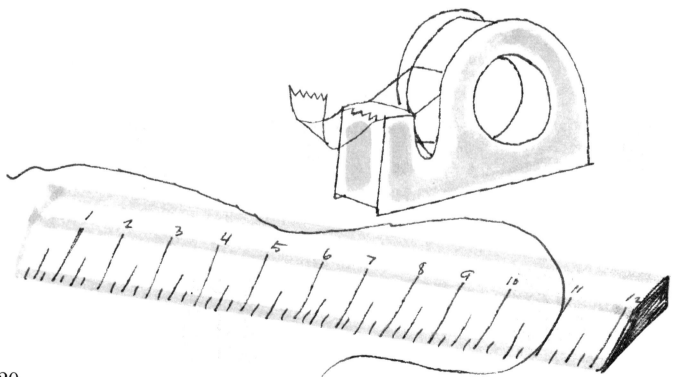

In the same way, you can hang a small rubber ball, or a small screwdriver, or a paintbrush from a hair. The hair will not break, because most ordinary hairs in good condition are strong enough to support two ounces of weight.

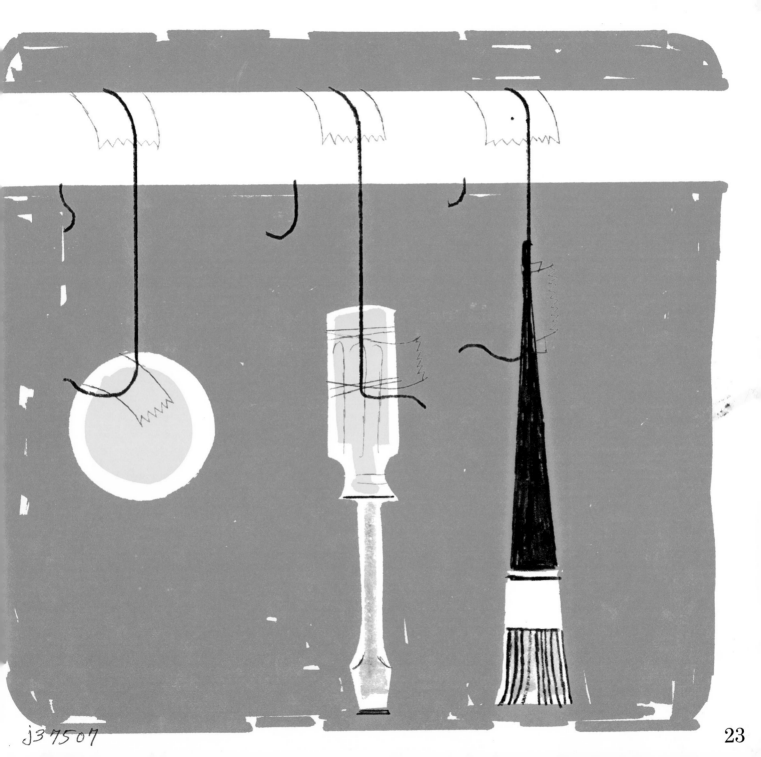

23

Hair is so strong that long ago the people of Japan used ropes made of many strands of hair to lift heavy loads.

Hair can stretch. You can prove this, too.
Get a large glass jar, a lid, a key, a hair, and some
   Scotch tape.

Tape the key to one end of the hair. Tape the other end of the hair firmly to the inside of the lid. Screw the lid onto the jar and mark the jar to show how far the key hangs down.

In one day, the hair will be longer, the key lower. If the hair was four inches long, it will stretch to about five inches.

Do the experiment again. This time put a small piece of damp sponge into the jar. Soon some of the moisture in the sponge will get into the air in the jar and then into the hanging hair. In four or five hours, the hair will become longer, and the key will hang lower.

When you grow up, you may curl your straight hair or straighten your curly hair. You may have your hair cut many times.

You may have your hair cut again and again. You may curl it or straighten it again and again. Every time it grows out, your hair will be your own kind of hair.

It will be straight if you have round follicles.

It will be a little curly if you have oval follicles.

It will be very curly if you have follicles that are shaped like little slots.

Look at your hair in the mirror.

Is it straight? Is it wavy?

Is it tight and curly?

Maybe you just had a summer haircut, and have no hair at all.

Don't worry. Your hair will grow in again. And when it does, it will be exactly the same as the hair you've had all along.

35

ABOUT THE AUTHOR

AUGUSTA GOLDIN was born in New York City but grew up on a farm in the Catskill Mountains near Ellenville, New York. She was graduated from Hunter College, received a Master of Science degree from the City University of New York, and an Ed.D. from Teachers College, Columbia University.

Mrs. Goldin has worked on the staffs of several education publications and is the principal of a school on Staten Island, New York. She has written several other Let's-Read-and-Find-Out science books.

ABOUT THE ILLUSTRATOR

When he is not writing or illustrating books, ED EMBERLEY pursues several interesting and unusual hobbies. He prints limited editions of children's books on his own hand press, studies Early Americana, and experiments with toy-making.

Mr. Emberley received a Bachelor of Fine Arts degree in illustration from the Massachusetts School of Art in Boston. He lives in Ipswich, Massachusetts.